GW00455295

Growing in Faith

BRINGING CHILDREN TO FAITH

Training adults in evangelism with children
Penny Frank

Contents

Text copyright © 2000 CPAS

This edition copyright © 2000 CPAS

First edition 2000

All rights reserved. The material in this book is copyright and may not be photocopied without permission from CPAS. However, the pages containing resources for group activities may be copied for use within the purchaser's own church.

Published by	Printed in conjunction with
CPAS	Scripture Union
Athena Drive	207-209 Queensway
Tachbrook Park	Bletchley
WARWICK	MILTON KEYNES
CV34 6NG	MK2 2EB
ISBN: 1 8976 6093 6	ISBN: 1 85999 410 5

Written by Penny Frank

Illustrated by Alex Hughes

Designed by ie Design

Edited by AD Publishing Services

Printed by Unigraph Printing Services

British Library Cataloguing-in-Publication Data

A catalogue record for this book is available from the British Library.

Church Pastoral Aid Society: Registered Charity No 1007820

A company limited by guarantee

Text on pages 40-44 'All God's Children'
© The Central Board of Finance of the Church of England 1991.
Reproduced by kind permission.

INTRODUCTION

Welcome to a book which I hope will be a doorway into evangelism with children. Its aim is to offer help both with the 'thinking about' and the 'doing' of bringing children to faith, so that the children in your area may hear about Jesus in an enjoyable and memorable way, and in a way which makes a difference to the whole of their lives.

Using this workbook

This book is intended to be a flexible and very practical resource. The chapters are divided into 'bite-sized chunks', and at the end of each chapter there is a one-page Group Focus which enables you to explore issues that have been raised in each chapter.

The first four chapters look broadly at the context for evangelism – the 'thinking about it' – and suggest ways in which people can prepare themselves for it. The next four chapters are more practical – the 'how to'. At the end of the workbook you will find a Resources section which will enable you to follow up any particular areas in more detail.

There are two main ways of using this workbook:

■ As a leader's training manual

Are you a leader who wants to focus on the key issues of children's evangelism? Perhaps you are responsible for leading a 'core group' within your church which has been given this responsibility. If so, working through the chapters on your own will give you the briefing you need before you begin working with your team. The Group Focus pages will help you to communicate the message of the book to your team members.

■ As a group resource

This book can also be used by a group of people who want to reach out to children in their area but don't know how to go about it. Each person in the group can work through the chapters individually and then use the Group Focus pages for group discussion.

A copy of the reports *All God's Children?* and *Children in the Way* will help as you do this work. Both are available through Church House Publishing. An adapted version of chapter 8 of

All God's Children? appears in the Resources section at the end of the book, which you may find useful and thought-provoking.

■ Head, heart and hands

Thinking through the subject of children and evangelism is not simply a cerebral exercise. Certainly, there is plenty for the mind to think about. But the heart needs to be stirred and new skills learned in order to do the job well. So this book is aimed not simply at the head, but at the heart and hands too. For this reason there will be points throughout the book where you will see signs like this ⊙ which will mean that it is time to stop reading in order to think, or pray, or do, something.

There are millions of children in the United Kingdom who have never heard the gospel. They stand little chance of being able to decide whether to live God's way or not; they don't know what God has said and done. They do not even know that they are people of his creation. They have a right to know and to decide for themselves.

When you are working as a group, take courage from each other as you explore the reality of what you want to do. The size of the task can seem daunting, but it really is worth doing. Stretch your imaginations as you discuss – don't just state the obvious. Look at God's word in depth rather than skimming over it – yes, it will be challenging but that is because evangelism is never simply about what God wants to do *through* us but also about what God wants to do *in* us. I pray that this workbook will help you reach out to many children. Go for it!

Penny Frank

REAL CHILDREN

Getting to know children is an important starting-point in talking with them about our faith. The most effective way of getting to know children is to spend significant time with them – time when we have nothing else to do but to be with them and to listen to them. The company of children can be exhausting and draining but it can also be stimulating and full of fun. One of the ways in which children relate to adults is in seeing them as providers of the answers to all their questions. This can be demanding!

Curiosity and children

A child asks questions in what often seems to be a random way. Questions can appear to have no connection with what is going on around them. A child can ask questions that cause embarrassment and unintentional hurt. A child's questions often make adults laugh.

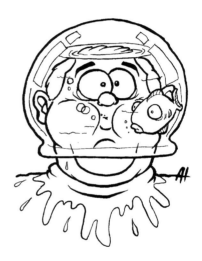

 THINK

Think back through your own childhood:

1. Who was your most memorable adult companion?
2. What did you enjoy about their company?
3. Was there anything that you did not enjoy about being with them?
4. What was the main way in which they gave you information?
5. What sort of questions did you ask them?

Here are some of the questions I can remember my own children asking me when they were small:

- Why does the water fall out of the tap in that shape?
- Why does the rain fall out of the clouds in bits?
- Why doesn't it come in the same shape as the water from the tap?
- Why does Daddy make that funny noise when he is asleep?
- Why can't I breathe water?
- Where does the dark go when you switch on the light?
- Why can't we keep the dark there all the time?
- Why does the plasticene go soft when you hold it in your hand?
- Why does pastry go hard when you put it in the oven?

- What do you call those things your ears hold up? (ear-rings)
- If you kiss my pillow will I feel it when you've gone out?

 REFLECT

1. What questions have you been asked by children?
2. What factors make answering children's questions difficult?
3. What can you do if you don't know the answer to a child's question?
4. How do you know when a child has been satisfied with your answer?
5. Why do you think adults ask fewer questions than children?

We often stop children asking questions because we are busy, or because we do not know the answers, or because the questions make us feel uncomfortable in some way. Children may embarrass us by asking questions in front of someone, or they may ask us questions that we have always wondered about ourselves! Children are not sophisticated in their understanding of an appropriate context for questions but usually simply think and then speak. Certainly living with small children as they go through the 'Why? What? Who? Where? How?' stage is exhausting; but this is the stage of most rapid development. This is because asking questions is one of the best ways of learning.

Curiosity and learning

Too often the 'educational' process of our lives involves being given information about which we have no curiosity. When this happens we do not retain the information unless we discipline ourselves to do so. On the other hand, if our reaction to some information is, 'Oh, I've always wanted to know that!' then the information is likely to stay in our memories with very little effort on our part to keep it there. If you are a gardener and someone tells you a foolproof formula for getting rid of greenfly, you will be anxious to get home in order to try it out and you will remember what the formula was. You had a question, someone told you the answer and you put it into practice and found it worked – you learnt something! The most challenging aspect of education is to stir up in a child curiosity about the information you want them to learn – before you teach them. We all need that 'Oh yes!' moment for learning to take place and the memory to be triggered.

⊜ REFLECT

1. What can you remember about the way in which you were educated?
2. How did you learn? Was it by having curiosity satisfied or learning by rote?
3. What stimulated your curiosity? Your surroundings? Other people? TV? Books?
4. Which subjects were hardest for you? Can you think why that was?
5. Did you have a lively imagination as a child? How did people respond to that?

◉ DO

In order to imagine the sort of questions which a small child might ask, place an ordinary, everyday object in front of you (or in the middle of the circle if there are several of you): for example, a watch, a candle floating in a glass, or a book. Set a kitchen timer for one minute and then ask out loud as many questions about that object as you can think of. You are not waiting for anyone to answer the questions (in a group you can all ask them at once). You are simply getting a feel for the flow of questions a child might have. When the timer goes, have a rough guess as to how many questions you managed. Then ask yourself what you think a child would have learnt if someone had been there to answer the questions.

> 'Many teachers increasingly spend time working not just as instructors but also with groups of children, drawing out their ideas and knowledge, helping them to extend and explore their experiences. The skills required for this approach to education are more demanding than those required for formal education.' (Children in the Way)

So why do we need all these special skills? Why not simply tell children what we want to tell them? Because what we want is for children to know God and to experience what the Christian life is like alongside us. We don't want them to be able to simply sit some sort of Scripture exam and be able to pass. The questions children ask are very important, both those which seem impossible to answer and those which seem trivial and naive. It is in the listening and answering of these questions, the way we help children to satisfy their curiosity and the way that we express our own, that learning takes place.

Answers to questions

We all know of people who continue to learn throughout their lives – newspapers love to feature an eighty-year-old with an Open University degree. But many of us fail to continue to learn once we are adult. Indeed, most adults stopped asking questions in their teens and have merely stayed within the pool of knowledge they already have. They rarely feel curious and they certainly don't allow themselves to express curiosity aloud in questions. Why does this happen?

■ **PROBLEM:** We learn to stop expressing curiosity if our questions are continually answered in an unsatisfactory way or ignored. So, if the only reaction a child gets when they ask a question is a grunt from

behind a newspaper or to be told to move from in front of the television they will soon stop bothering to ask them.

- **SOLUTION:** More one-to-one conversational opportunities between adult and child.

- **PROBLEM:** We learn to stop expressing curiosity if our questions are always met with derision by either adults or our peer group. If we seriously want to know, but all our questions ever produce is laughter, we will soon not bother to ask them.

- **SOLUTION:** However young a child is, they know when you are laughing at them. We need to discipline ourselves to take a question seriously and then perhaps to enjoy a good laugh in privacy afterwards – and to be careful who we talk to about the episode.

- **PROBLEM:** We learn to stop asking questions when the adults around us are seen as the ones who only answer questions and neither ask their own nor say 'I don't know' in answer to ours. Not asking questions, or appearing to know all the answers, becomes synonymous with being grown-up (for some reason, people go through childhood wanting to be grown-up!).

- **SOLUTION:** We need to learn alongside our children and express our wonder or curiosity with them. We need to be able to say 'I don't know – what do you think about that?' and

not to feel that we have lost face by doing so. We need to know what to do with difficult questions and where to start to explore the possible answers.

One of the most rewarding ways of exploring truth with children is to extend a conversation for as long as possible before coming to a conclusion. This means that you will need to use good listening skills – regular eye contact and reassuring comments. It also means that when a question is asked by the child, you will need to be disciplined enough not to give an answer but rather to say:

- 'What's your own opinion about that?'
- 'I've always wondered about that too!'
- 'Yes, that's strange, isn't it?'
- 'I wonder how we could find out?'

If you pursue the conversation in this way, you will find that the conversation has covered far more ground than a simple question and answer would have done. You will have got to know each other better. You will have gained a far deeper insight into the way in which a child's mind works.

Group Focus:
understanding children and their world

Understanding the link between curiosity and learning is an important one for us, if we want to become involved in evangelism with children. All too often the 'answers' given by the church address questions which people are simply not asking! The big challenge for us as we reach out to children is how to stimulate and satisfy a child's curiosity about God in a way that allows them safe opportunities to explore personal faith. It can seem a daunting challenge. Here are some suggestions of ways in which your skills and confidence can be grown.

Role play

In pairs, hold a conversation which must not come to a conclusion for three minutes. One of you takes the role of the child and the other of the adult listener. Set a subject like 'Watching *Blue Peter*' or 'A visit to the zoo'. The child can express as much curiosity as they like. The role of the adult is to listen and to choose which questions to offer an answer to; and which questions to use in order to extend the conversation by turning them back to the child. If the child seems to get stuck then the adult can throw in a question in order to restart it. Talk afterwards carefully about the skills of the listening adult and any frustrations of the child.

Visit

Some people who want to work with children in evangelism have not been inside a primary school since they left as a child. The school is an important place for seeing children in context and for getting a good picture of the abilities and attitudes of children today. It may be possible to approach a local school with an official letter from your church and arrange to spend some time there observing. Explain to the school that you want to understand children better and to see them in context; be open to any suggestions they might make about how you could spend time while you are there. You will learn far more by being unnoticeable because you are clearing up the library than if you sit with your pen and notebook! Meet together afterwards with others in your group and talk through the differences between what you expected and what you actually saw.

A child's world

Ask members of the group to do some research beforehand, and then spend an evening together, each person contributing something to help you explore a child's world. Everyone will benefit from the research, and all of you will learn something new! The contributions could be:

- a video of a popular film; or record some children's TV programmes
- examples of children's computer games
- children's books and magazines
- children's music on CD or tapes.

Of course, the term 'children' covers an enormous difference in age-range from three to eleven years old. For those under the age of three, we would use the terms 'toddler' or 'baby'; and certainly from twelve years old the label of 'child' will not be welcomed! So when you bring your contribution to the group it is important to define what age child you are talking about – you may decide to bring examples across the age-range in each category.

At the end of your group time give everyone the opportunity to suggest ways in which this unit has changed their knowledge of, or attitudes to, the world of children. How will those changes enable you to feel more confident as you prepare to talk to children about Jesus?

REAL EVANGELISM

Starting point

The starting point of any evangelism is our own faith. First, we need to know what the gospel is ourselves and to understand how the Bible encourages us to spread the good news in evangelism. Evangelism is bringing people face to face with Jesus Christ because he died for them. It is showing people the way to God the Father through preaching Jesus, by the power of the Holy Spirit. It is confronting people with his name, his teaching, his promises, his life, his death, his resurrection and his kingdom. We are not able to do that unless we ourselves have been changed by that truth and are still excited by it. Some people get involved in evangelism because they feel guilty about spreading their faith and feel that they have to. Please do not do any evangelism if guilt is your motivation. Evangelism with children is important for all the same reasons that it is important for all other people. Children need to hear the gospel because everyone does.

THINK

Read through Matthew 28:16-20.

- Does Jesus solely mean adults when he sends his disciples to make more disciples?
- If we exclude children from the Great Commission then will we also exclude those with disability? Those who cannot understand through lack of education? Those who cannot contribute because they are poor? Those we do not understand because of race? Male and female?

As soon as we start excluding people we don't know where to stop. 'Make disciples' must mean telling the good news to everyone, and that must include children. Just think! There were no doubt adults in the early church who as children had seen and listened to Jesus.

Evangelism with children also gives them a chance to become involved in evangelism themselves. Christian children need our encouragement to tell the gospel to their peer group. However, it's no good telling children to spread the news about Jesus to their friends if there is no appropriate activity in our church for their friends to come to. We will simply leave them feeling confused, even guilty. If we provide for their friends in our evangelism, we also need to look at the provision we make for child evangelists.

When we think of the children in our church who want to evangelize their friends, we should ask ourselves these questions:

- Have we taught our children the Bible? That is, not simply a few basic Bible stories but the big story of God and the application of the story to their lives?
- Have we modelled the Christian life to them?
- Have they had the opportunity to express doubts, difficulties, spiritual hunger themselves or have we taught them to keep these things out of the way? If they haven't learnt how to deal with their own questions, they are unlikely to cope very well with the questions of their friends.
- Have we taught them what the Bible teaches about sin, forgiveness, punishment and the life of the Spirit?
- Do they know about, and are they prepared for, the attack from the enemy of God?

Children need to hear the whole truth and not a watered-down or pulped version of it – they need to hear it because everyone needs to. The church needs to exercise the skill of explaining the gospel to children, and that skill needs to be in evidence in the children already in the church, before reaching out to those who are not yet in the church.

Children's spirituality

Children grow spiritually just as they develop in other ways – through steady, slow, almost imperceptible progress. That growth will happen – just as their feet continue to grow even if that growth is ignored. But, just as their feet will become misshapen if they wear the wrong size shoes, so their faith will be misshapen (even wither and die) if it is ignored.

A child's spirituality is nurtured by many things. The key factors are their core relationships and values: if they relate in satisfying and loving relationships with those around them, they will be secure and open to grow into other relationships too. If, within those core relationships, a high value is placed on qualities like honesty, compassion, fun, appreciation of creation and the arts, then the spirit of the child will flourish and grow. Children can respond with awe and wonder to beauty and order in what sometimes seems to be the most unlikely ways.

REFLECT

One small boy, Gary, was renowned for making life difficult for both himself and for those around him. It was always a relief when he was not in school. One day his teacher had an observation jar in the classroom with greenfly and ladybirds on some leafy twigs. Gary spent the entire day holding the jar and watching the ladybirds with their captive meal. No one really minded that they could not have a look or get anywhere near the jar because Gary was so quiet and trouble-free. At the end of the day he was the one who took the jar outside and with a look of wonder let the ladybirds fly free.

REFLECT

Sheena responded to the following poem by Walter de la Mare:

> Slowly, silently, now the moon
> Walks the night in her silver shoon;
> This way, and that, she peers, and sees
> Silver fruit upon silver trees;
> One by one the casements catch
> Her beams beneath the silvery thatch;
> Couched in his kennel, like a log,
> With paws of silver sleeps the dog;

From their shadowy cote the white breasts peep
Of doves in a silver-feathered sleep;
A harvest mouse goes scampering by,
With silver claws, and silver eye;
And moveless fish in the water gleam,
By silver reeds in a silver stream.

('Silver', from *The Complete Poems of Walter de la Mare*, 1969 (USA: 1970), by permission of the Literary Trustees of Walter de la Mare, and the Society of Authors as their representative)

'This poem describes moonlight how I imagine it, all slow and silent but with just a bit of movement which is the harvest mouse. I also like the poem because it is mysterious and it makes me feel, when I look at the moon, that it is looking back at me. The last few lines of the poem make me say them quietly, and when I have finished I'm very silent like the moon (much to Mum's relief!).'

A child's reaction to space is to run into it and try to fill it. Their response to water and sand is to become part of it. They are noisy when loud music plays and quiet when the music is soft. They easily become engrossed in paint, scissors and glue, clay and dough. What they produce is part of them – they are heart-broken when their work is spoiled or ridiculed. The mark of a creator God is etched deeply in their lives, giving us the amazing challenge of nurturing their spiritual development in many ways.

Faith development

The growth of faith – not to be confused with spirituality – can happen alongside and be part of the development of the spirit. Unfortunately, in our culture, faith is often seen as something which develops only within organized religion; and spirituality comes a poor second. When we plan and prepare for evangelism with children, it is important that we are confident about how faith can grow and how a child's spirituality can be nurtured.

There has been a great deal of research into the ways in which faith develops. The patterns which emerge can help us in our planning and understanding, but it is important also to remember that the psychologists who did the research did not feel that they had come to a final conclusion. In fact, they often returned to their research with different conclusions.

Based on the foundational thinking of psychologists Piaget and Kohlberg, James Fowler is the leading psychologist in the research about development of faith. Piaget discerned stages in the way we think and Kohlberg in the way we make moral judgements. Fowler went on from there to plot out six different stages of faith. He called these:

- **Stage 1:** Chaotic Faith. Fowler looked for this stage to be experienced somewhere between the ages of three and eight. The 'chaos' is permitted by the child's unordered imagination that produces unreasoned thinking with powerful images.
- **Stage 2:** Ordered Faith. Fowler saw the age-range for this as between six and twelve years old. Here the child can hold a reasoned line of thinking and can sort out some of the chaos of the earlier stages.
- **Stage 3**: Conforming Faith. This stage can start as early as eleven and persists for many adults throughout their lives. In this stage people are able to think abstractly and to see their thoughts in relation to others and the way in which they think.
- **Stage 4:** Choosing Faith. Here people want their faith to be personal; something which they have opted for themselves. They want to make their own decisions about faith, do their own learning and find their own way forward in life on the basis of that faith.
- **Stage 5:** Balanced Faith. Fowler thought this was unlikely to be arrived at before the middle years of adulthood. This is a more inclusive faith and loses some of the unity and neatness of the earlier faith but with an added richness because a person at this stage of faith is able to hold more possible options together in their faith without feeling the need to tidy it up.
- **Stage 6:** Selfless Faith. Fowler saw this as a rare stage for anyone to go through. He saw examples in people like Mother Teresa or Martin Luther King of people where 'the circle of their love and their recognition of community has widened to include the whole human race'.

Fowler concluded that people moved through these, or some of these, stages and that each move forwards alternated with a period of stability. Not everyone will go through all of these stages, since not everyone progresses to a stage of mature development in their faith. Nor is every transition smooth, since progress can be triggered by a crisis or sudden injection of new thought.

James Westerhoff adopted Fowler's thinking and to some extent popularized it. Although he did no further research of his own, he suggested four styles of faith, each one distinct from the other. He compared the growth of faith to the rings of growth in a tree trunk, seeing us expanding from one stage of faith to another, containing within ourselves all the previous stages – just as a tree is always completely a tree and always containing the earlier growth and rings of development.

Westerhoff called these rings:

- **experienced** – the active and responding faith of early years which centres around key human relationships
- **affiliative** – faith experienced by belonging to groups and recognizing the authority of the community in which the group exists
- **searching** – the questions and experimentation of later youth are typical of this stage; while they give the impression of instability, they are actually important
- **owned faith** – this brings the previous stages into a productive and effective faith which comes from within but is also outward-looking.

As we embark on children's evangelism, it helps us to see that there are stages of development of faith to go through. The stage a child or adult is in will determine their reaction and response to the gospel. Children who come to our events will all be different in their looks and temperament; they will also be different in their response to God and to the gospel. But there are also differences in response that are linked with their age. It is not reasonable to expect a child's reaction and response to be that of an adult. Nor is it reasonable to expect the response of a three-year-old to be the same as that of a ten-year-old. Whatever their age, their response is not less or inferior – simply different.

Group Focus:
spirituality and faith development

Although we have all journeyed through stages of faith development ourselves, it is hard to look back and to transfer our feelings *then* into our experience as a leader or children's evangelist *now*. Working through this page will help you bridge the gap between your adult faith and that of the child.

Story time

Take this opportunity to hear how you each came to faith in Christ. Give each person plenty of time so that you can ask questions and listen to whole stories.

- Are there any similarities in the stories?
- What are the major differences?
- What part have childhood experiences played in bringing you to faith?
- Stop after each story and pray for the person who has told the story.
- Praise God for his work of grace in each of your lives.

Look at Deuteronomy 11

1. Collect together everything in this chapter which refers directly to children.
2. How does the rest of the chapter relate to children?
3. Sum up what you think God's attitude towards children is in this chapter.

Read Romans 1:2-6

1. How would you describe the gospel with the help of these verses?
2. How would you describe evangelism with the help of these verses?

Look at Luke 15:1-7

Think of some of the things that you would find hard about telling this story to children. What would you enjoy about being the storyteller? How would your approach differ if the children you were talking to were:

- all from Christian homes
- all from non-Christian homes

- in a school assembly
- listening to you one-to-one?

Many children experience the spiritual in creative activity. Tick which of these experiences you enjoy and would want to enable children to enjoy. Would any of them be spiritual experiences for you?

- painting
- modelling with clay or dough
- drawing or colouring
- collecting natural objects to make a picture
- listening to music

- making music
- watching dance
- dancing
- walking, climbing and clambering
- being with small animals
- taking photos
- using model-making toys
- cutting and sticking
- drama and mime.

At the end of your group time give everyone the opportunity to suggest ways in which your discussion has changed their knowledge of, or attitudes to, the world of children. How will those changes enable you to feel more confident as you prepare to talk to children about Jesus?

REAL WORLD

Society

What is society? Who defines what it is? How do we know whether it is influencing us for good or ill? How does it influence children?

Society is the context in which we live. It is all around us as we live in our street, shop in our supermarket, are educated in our schools, watch our television and read our papers. Its influence is there in our friendships and reflected in our lives by what we wear, how we talk, the values we have and the choices we make. We are each a tiny microcosm of our society from the moment we are born, and particularly as we move outside our families to go to playgroup, school, church, and later the world of work.

Society is the context for all our evangelism. Often the church is perceived as a place apart – a community which supports another society, different from the one inhabited by everyone else in the world. When people join the church they often feel they are joining another society, rather than learning to live more deeply or differently in the real one. That is a challenge for us.

The Bible tells us that God's kingdom is 'not of this world' and that his kingdom has come among us. The values of God's kingdom are different from those of our modern world – they are 'people values' not 'product values', they are to do with the real heart of the matter and not with outward appearances. Does this mean that the gospel cannot be heard by people in our society – is the language and approach too different to be communicated across the divide?

The interesting thing is that society changes. It is not static: it changes around us without our consent or our design. That change is influenced by all sorts of factors, some of which can easily be assessed and others which are imperceptible. Think of the difference the computer has made to society over the last ten years. The change is enormous; it has made a huge impact on education and industry, commerce and family life – in fact, on every area of life.

Children are part of our society and are particularly vulnerable to its impact and influence – they have seen less change than we have and it is the only form of society they have

ever known. If we do not seem to belong to society as they understand it, and appear to 'mis-fit' in it, our message will also seem to belong to a world other than theirs. Their culture of music, books, television programmes, education, ways of communicating, kinds of dance and the process of relating to each other is part of the society we inhabit but will never be our culture. We will never know what it is like to be a child in the new millennium but we do need to make an effort to *try* to imagine what it might be like.

The family

The expression and structure of family life has seen huge changes over the last generation. More parents are bringing up families on their own, and more children are having to come to terms with parents who live in different places with different partners and all the attendant challenges that gives them.

⊘ THINK

Think back through your own family life as a child:

- What was the relationship like between your parents?
- What other siblings did you have and what was your relationship with them?
- Was the family in any way 'extended', and if so by whom?
- What was the family attitude to money?
- What was the family attitude to sex?
- What was the family attitude to faith/religion?

Now take a look at your life in the present day and notice the various ways in which that background has influenced the way you think and live. Look especially at the way it has influenced how you think and feel about your faith.

It is important that when we talk to children about God we don't use analogies of family life that mean nothing because they have never experienced them. This does not mean that we cannot teach the truth about God as a 'loving Father' as some people maintain, 'because these children do not know what a loving father is'. Indeed, you can argue that these children need to meet with their Father God more than any other! But it is no good simply depending and drawing on that experience in the way you teach and tell a story. You will then be giving them a message that this good news is not for people like them.

Even though many of the children who come to the evangelistic events you arrange will be from your church, not all Christian families function in the same way:

- Some Christian families are silent about their faith and would never discuss it at home.
- Some Christian parents live very differently in the home from the way they are in church, and children become confused and hurt by their hypocrisy.
- Others may be very committed to the

Christian way of life and their children may feel under pressure to perform in a certain way.

So, when starting any sort of evangelism with children, think about their families. For all sorts of reasons, it is well worth taking the time to get to know their families: make the opportunity to visit their homes – just briefly with an invitation or a leaflet is enough to give you an insight into the family setting. Invite parents to come to see what you are doing with, and saying to, their children. It's usually better to invite them to come informally so that they see the event as it really is rather than on a special parents' occasion when it will all feel like a performance. Find out if the church has links with any other part of the family or has had opportunities to serve the family in weddings or funerals. All these links are important and can be built on as you reach out to the family in children's evangelism.

School

School, of course, is the main outside influence on the life of a child under ten. Each day a child spends six or seven hours being moulded by the atmosphere and philosophy of their school. No wonder that when a child quotes someone's opinion to you that person is likely to be connected to their school!

Keeping good links with local schools is important when you are involved in evangelism with children. This can not only give an immediate insight into the life of children in your area, but also allow you to build up a relationship between church and school, which may then lead to opportunities to go into school to take an assembly. Knowing the school also gives you some helpful idea before you start about the level of discipline the children are used to – and that could be really useful!

⊙ FIND OUT

How the local school operates will have an immediate impact on your evangelism among local children. If the school gives easy access to parents at any time of the school day, then you can expect parents to be prepared to come onto your church premises easily and to get involved. But if the school discourages parents from setting foot on the school premises except by appointment, you may well find you have to work hard as a team to make contact with the parents. You will need actually to invite them in when they bring children, or to insist that they collect the child from a certain part of the building at the end of an event.

How the school functions will not only affect your relationship with the children but will also have implications for your events: if the children are accustomed in school to having their opinions sought and listened to, then you will probably find them ready to talk in small groups. But in some schools where staff are struggling (with poor premises or a difficult catchment area, for example) the teachers may well find themselves more intent on being listened to than in listening.

It is also worth finding out details about the curriculum in the school by chatting to a teacher about it. Find out what your local school chooses to do over and above the demands of the National Curriculum. From this you will know what sort of activities the children may be interested in, and it will give you a clearer idea of how likely the children are to contribute to particular activities. (The types of activities you might be interested in running are discussed in more detail in Chapter 5.)

◉ Do

Do some local research in swimming pools, theatres and sports centres to see which are the popular activities and to see whether you can link into these what you offer in your event. For example, if the school has a lively attitude towards drama and music but little space for sport, you can expect quite a high level of contribution towards music and drama, but any sport workshops would probably be especially popular. You could use your visit to families to do some research into children's activities – but remember always to carry with you authorization from your minister to make your visit official.

Group Focus:
the real world of the child

Here are some ideas for getting the feel of the society in which you live and the culture to which your local children belong. They are suggestions which will take some time and effort but they may be activities which you could do over a period of time – not all at once before moving on to the next chapter!

The influence

In chapter 1 I encouraged you to begin to experience the culture of the child by looking at some of the things which influence them. Continue to do that – perhaps ordering their magazines regularly and watching some of their programmes every week. There is no short-cut way to learn how children think and live; it takes time and effort. We will never be children again but we can learn to speak so that they hear us and understand what we are saying. With a message like ours it is worth the effort.

Read chapter 8 of the report 'All God's Children?'

This chapter has been printed at the back of this workbook, starting on page 40. This gives answers to some of the important questions about the gospel and children's culture and offers some recommendations for churches that are getting involved in evangelism with children. Reading this may help give you a structure for your local research.

Workshops

Make a list of all the possible workshop or interest groups which you think you could run for children through your church. Then work on a list of similar activities that are popular with the children in your area. Edit both lists as you find out more about the children's interests and as other members join your group planning evangelism.

Watch television together

Tape a couple of episodes of *The Simpsons*:

- What shocks you?
- What makes you laugh?
- What do you not understand?
- How true to life do you think it is?
- Why do you think it is so popular?

Read Matthew 18:1-14 and 19:13-15

Notice where the story of the Lost Sheep comes in this Gospel.

- What do you notice in Jesus' attitude to children in these passages?
- Where do you feel most challenged?
- Where do you feel most encouraged?
- Pray together for schools in your area.
- Pray together for the families you are going to start to contact.
- Pray for each other as God prepares you for this work.

At the end of your group time give everyone the opportunity to suggest ways in which this Group Focus has changed their knowledge of, or attitudes to, the world of children. How will those changes enable you to feel more confident as you prepare to talk to children about Jesus?

REAL GOD

The Trinity

Many children relate to a hidden secret friend – someone they share their most intimate fears and worries with and someone who is with them wherever they are. This is quite normal and they grow out of it, but it is a very real experience while it lasts. For a child, the world of the seen and the unseen are not clearly separated. They find it hard to make the distinction between fact and fiction, truth and imagination, things they have done and those they have only dreamed of doing. They find it hard because the world of their minds is as real as the world of their eyes.

Despite this, many people in the church worry about teaching children about the three persons of the Trinity rather than simply about Jesus. They say, 'Children can imagine Jesus because of the Gospels but they cannot imagine the Father or the Spirit.' This is not necessarily logical. What *is* true, however, is that the person of the Trinity we find easiest to communicate to a child is the one we ourselves relate to most easily.

THINK

Delve into your own mind for a moment:

- What do you think Jesus looked like while he was on earth?
- What do you think Jesus looks like now?
- What do you imagine when you pray to God the Father?
- Which person of the Trinity do you most usually address when you pray?
- Do you ever pray to the Spirit?
- What picture do you have in your mind when you talk to the Spirit?
- When you imagine heaven, which of those three persons of the Trinity are you expecting to meet?

What you think, feel and imagine makes a lot of difference to what you are happy to teach and tell. If I usually pray to Jesus, then it is likely that I will be most comfortable with the 'image' of Jesus and will therefore tend to introduce him to the children in my home and my group. This means that I will usually tell stories about Jesus, address my prayers in the group to Jesus and encourage children to do the same by the way I introduce the prayer time. This is unfortunately the way in which a lot of youth and children's work is done.

The Trinity does not exist to give us a range of gods from which to choose or in order to cater for our different preferences when we approach God. The fact is that there is one God and we need to be very careful to teach that truth about him right from the beginning in evangelism.

THINK AGAIN

1. How do you imagine God the Father?

   When I was a child I used to imagine God the Father sitting with a newspaper so that he could be with me all the time – after all, he would have to do something to pass the time when I wasn't talking to him.

2. How do you imagine God the Son?

   I imagined Jesus only as arms/hands which helped/comforted/punished/lifted me up to see God and, for some reason, conducted the choirs of angels. I can remember how well the angels had done on Christmas Eve with their usual conductor in a manger.

3. How do you imagine God the Holy Spirit?

   I always imagined the Holy Spirit as beautiful perfume.

The Bible teaches the Trinity as a wonderful truth and we need to think through how we introduce children to God in all his intimate majesty.

The Holy Spirit

We may well rise to the challenge of teaching God the Father and God the Son. But for many people it is likely to be God the Holy Spirit who gets left out. Most adults have found the Spirit to be the most difficult person of the Trinity to understand, so they feel that children certainly will not understand. Perhaps we feel that his coming in Acts with rushing wind and flames of fire, strange tongues and impassioned preaching is a confusing image. Or maybe we are confused by the present-day presentation of the Spirit where people seem to attribute to God the Holy Spirit any weird and strange thing happening in the church. In fact, I think that children understand the Spirit most easily.

THINK

Pause for a moment and consider how the Spirit of God works in your own life. These are the ways in which I recognize the work of the Spirit in my life:

- When I realize that I want to see God at work in my life: my natural desire is away from God but the Holy Spirit gives me the desire for God and for his word (John 4:24).
- When I realize that I want to pray: the Holy Spirit is the one who is drawing me to communicate with God and to listen to him (Romans 8:15).
- When I realize that I have discernment about a person or a subject – the sudden feeling of 'Where did that come from?' as I express an opinion which seems very clear and obvious to me (Ephesians 1:17).
- When my family, friends and church leaders recognize the Holy Spirit at work in my life. This may happen at different times and ways (2 Corinthians 3:18).
- When I look back on my life – perhaps at New Year, my birthday or at the anniversary of my conversion (Galatians 5:16).
- As I encourage myself with the fact that every time I recognize God working anywhere, at that moment I am experiencing the work of his Spirit in my life.
- Because I know that I am in the kingdom of God (Romans 8:16).

So, as you look down that list of very ordinary things which you will have added to from your own experience, you must ask yourself this question: 'Is there anything there which is unsuitable or inappropriate for children?' Surely we would want children to enjoy everything on the above list? But for them to do so, they need

to be introduced to the person of God the Holy Spirit so that they recognize God at work through the Spirit in their lives and praise God for it.

Often the concern of adults about the Holy Spirit and children is that God will give gifts and experiences to the child which they, the adult, are not used to and they won't know how to react. I think that concern needs to rest with God. What we must do is to teach the Bible to children in evangelism, be ready to answer questions as honestly as we can and pray that God the Spirit will work in and through our lives. If we do those three things, I am confident that God hears prayer and will work in the lives of children in a way which is both significant and appropriate for them.

Prayer

When we introduce children to prayer in the course of evangelism we probably veer in one of two directions: we either want to discourage children from praying for anything where the answers can be measured (that is, they will know whether God has said 'yes' or 'no'); or we want them to pray for the miraculous every time. Which of these categories we fall into depends on our own theology of prayer and also on our own temperament.

Rather than taking one of these routes, what we actually need to do first of all is to encourage children to talk to God and to listen to God. If we do that, they will then make their own decisions about what to pray and how to pray.

This, of course, can still present us with problems. Children may come to us and ask us to pray about something which is not in keeping with Bible teaching and the character of God. What do we do then?

We can ask them some gentle questions like these:

■ What do you think God will feel as he listens to that prayer?
■ What do you think God is wanting to say to you about that situation even before you pray about it?
■ What do you think God is saying to you about you before you start to pray?

These questions can often help children to start to see things from another point of view and to start to pray to God with God in mind, rather than treating prayer like a press button in the Science Museum!

It is good to encourage children to keep a record of some of their prayers and of the answers they have had. Encourage them also to keep a record of what they have heard when they have spent time listening to God. Give them opportunity to do this during your evangelistic events – prayer is not an add-on experience later on when they are in the regular groups in church.

We ourselves must model and encourage honesty in prayer. God does not need us to bolster his image as an 'Answerer of Prayers'. We need to help children to be honest about the answers:

■ the ones they celebrate
■ the ones they do not understand
■ the ones that seem to be the opposite of what they asked.

Children need to be encouraged to go on thinking as they pray and not to assume that they will still be praying for exactly the same thing in six months' time. They need to be helped to see that, as they pray about a situation, God is talking to them about it and helping them to see it from his perspective.

Finally, prayer is not an adult thing which children only play at. Adults pray and children pray – it's the same thing. The only things which are different about children is that they are shorter physically, have less experience and a smaller vocabulary. God needs none of those things in order to hear and answer prayer. So encourage the children to pray for you and for other adults. Encourage them to pray for each other, and always emphasize that prayer is both speaking and listening.

Group Focus:
the challenge of teaching the truth about God

Here is a personal story to read together in your group. It is an example of how a child can understand and visualize spiritual truth.

The dream

First of all, sit quietly with your eyes closed. Then ask one person to read this account of a child's dream aloud while the rest of the group keep their eyes closed and imagine the dream happening.

'When I was eight or nine years old and had recently been taken to Horse Guards' Parade in London, I had this "waking dream":

I was running across a parade ground in total panic and fear. I could see a group of vicious people with stones and I knew that they were out to get me. There was no escape. The only person with me was someone I presumed to be my father – he had taken me to Horse Guards' Parade – and as the situation reached an unbelievable peak of fear, he pulled me round from beside him to stand behind him and underneath his overcoat.

I put my arms round his waist and hung on to the belt of his trousers so that I kept with him as he continued to run. Then I felt us turn as he faced the inevitable conflict. I could feel the sweat of his body and the heaving of his breath as he flinched. I could hear the crash of the stones the assailants were throwing and saw them roll past us on the ground beneath the overcoat. He groaned and swayed and at last crumpled and fell. I lay under the coat and I knew he was dead. I was crying and hot under the coat.

Everything was quiet, so I crawled out and looked around. The parade ground was empty and unthreatening. The path towards which I had been heading, when disaster struck, now offered free access. The tears still ran down my face as I looked down at the dead body of the man.

Then I saw that the coat was empty and he was standing there laughing down at me. Not my father after all but another all-powerful, unable-to-be-beaten Saviour. He swung me round him and we were both laughing as we ran towards the path.'

READ

Now look up Romans 5 and read it through together.

READ ON

This is not a fictional dream: ten years later when the members of the youth group I belonged to studied Romans 5, that picture leapt back into my mind. I relived the memory with Christ as the figure who rescued me. I felt again the fear and total helplessness and I felt the strength of that arm as he swung me away from danger and under his cloak – my sin under his righteousness. I felt the agony of that death as he faced it with my dead weight hanging round him. I saw again the huge granite rocks, that were meant for me, rolling past my feet when he had taken their blow. I felt again the body slump in death as I rolled to the ground beside him in the overcoat. I lived again the moment of exhilarating joy as I was swung round by a living Lord. I did not understand my 'free gift' but was so exceedingly thankful for it. The words in Romans 5:6 'For when we were still powerless, Christ died for the ungodly' and Romans 5:9 'saved from God's wrath through him' became powerfully evocative statements as I relived my childhood dream.

That dream taught me biblical truth as a child when I was too young to be able to read and understand the book of Romans for myself. It paved the way for the written word of God to have an impact on my life later on. This has influenced how I feel and think about the way in which God and children interact.

DISCUSS

- What were your observations and feelings as you read or heard this story?
- Have you had similar thoughts or dreams as a child?
- Have you listened to any children talking about what they think or imagine in a way that reminds you of this dream?
- What sort of truths do you think children can understand if they are illustrated appropriately?

SETTINGS FOR EVANGELISM

There are so many different ways in which to reach out to children with the gospel, but only certain ways will be appropriate for the children in our particular area. It is important that we do not look at a model which has been successful in one church and lift it straight into our own situation. Nor should we think that if we get hold of the right person, or the right material, then that will guarantee our success. As we look at the lives of the children in our area we will need to put together a plan and process which is just right for them.

First thoughts and prayer

Two of the major influences on the life of a child are family and school. If parents or teachers in your area have negative attitudes towards the work of your church, then you are likely to have an uphill struggle. But if, for whatever reason, they are in favour of the work you do, then you are likely to see some success. When you start to pray about evangelism, start by praying for parents and schools, rather than simply praying for the children and their response. The attitudes held by the adults are the attitudes that their children hold also.

 THINK

Take a moment to look at this list of different forms of evangelism:

- family evangelism
- friendship evangelism
- regular groups
- regular church services
- special services at the festivals
- children's home groups
- an all-age mission
- holiday Bible club
- Christian holidays
- events in schools.

All of these kinds of evangelism, except perhaps friendship evangelism, need a team of people. If you, as an individual, want to start a programme of children's evangelism in your area, one of the important things is to start with a group of people to do local research and make decisions about what kind of evangelism would be appropriate. Please do not decide what you are going to do and how you are going to do it and then ask people to back you in it. Instead, ensure that four or five people are praying, thinking and making decisions with you so that a core group is working on this from the beginning. Those of us who work with children sometimes have a bad reputation for going off and doing our own thing. Even if some of us feel that our church tends not to be interested in what we do with children, it is very unhealthy to try to run the show on our own. The rest of our church needs to know what we are doing because our ministry with children belongs to the whole church not just to one or two people.

The church

One question needs addressing before you start: is your children's evangelism going to be a 'stand-alone' one-off special event or an on-going series which is woven into the general life of the church? There is no right or wrong answer!

The answer will depend on resources and needs: how many leaders and what sort of budget your church has as well as the needs of the local children. You may decide that as children's leaders you are stretched to provide for those you already have, that you have no spare children's leaders and that your budget will pay only for one special event each year and not for a whole new club meeting every week. Or you may decide that there is such a shortage of out-of-school activities for children in your area that you need to provide a regular event, such as an after-school club, for them.

Either way, decide how this evangelism will fit into the rest of the work you do with children in your church. How might an annual special event be linked with the week-by-week contact you already have with children from church families? What will be the attitude of, and the level of involvement offered by, your church towards this special event? Who will be the leaders to run it? Don't presume that the leaders who serve in the regular children's groups will be the ones to do the evangelism. They may not have time for that as well.

Another question is whether you see evangelism and the 'nurture' of children in your regular church groups as two different strands of children's work in your church. If so, it is very important to keep the regular leaders well informed. They could feel that you are having all the fun and getting everyone's interest while they are slogging away with the church children, but with little ongoing support.

◐ THINK

What are some of the activities and clubs which you could run in order to communicate the gospel to children? Some examples are:

■ **special events at Easter, Pentecost or Christmas** – lasting a week, a series of evenings or one Saturday
■ **a holiday Bible club** which operates on four or five consecutive days of a school holiday – mornings or just afternoons; or a day which offers group work in the mornings and games in the afternoon
■ **an after-school club:** this could offer shelter for homework and care for those children whose parents go out to work. It could also provide a mixture of teaching aid, television supervision, craft and games. The 'evangelism' could happen on, say, one evening a week, or daily at, for example, a break for refreshments.

■ **special interest events on Saturday mornings** – for example, one week sport, the next computers, another crafts and a fourth videos. Each would provide cover and care for children at a time when parents would be glad of the help. An opportunity for telling the good news could be built into the morning when you break for refreshments.

The important principle is that the evangelism is

an integral part of your local church – whatever form it takes. Whether you have events during the week, or during school holidays, or only once a year, they are part of the life of your church. Church members need to be informed well in advance, so they can own it and pray for you. When it goes well, they need to feel they have achieved something, whether directly involved or not. When it goes through difficulties, as it certainly will, they need to pray for you as though it is happening to them.

Families

The families in your church are one of the key features of church life that will directly affect the success of evangelism with children: if those who already have children and teenagers in the church are committed to drawing other families in, then anything you do with children is almost bound to succeed. In this situation you can guarantee that you will be backed up by your church members.

Families will also provide the starting-point for any special event – they are the ones who have the contacts with children on the fringe of your church. For example, you could decide that to help this flow of contact and invitation you will lead into the holiday club with a series of special all-age services to which families can invite other families. Explain to your church families that this is part of the process, and encourage them to invite families to come. If you do not have a tradition of all-age services at your church you could hold the initial one for church families, lasting forty to fifty minutes which carefully and specifically teaches one passage of the Bible in a fast-moving and memorable way. Keep it simple and focused. At the end of the service explain that this will be the format of the next three all-age services, which you would like them to invite another family along to. Provide them with invitations for these services which give snappy titles indicating what each one is going to be about.

At these services you can introduce your new initiative in children's evangelism. The parents who have come to these services will then have some degree of trust in what you are going to do and how you are going to do it. They will know who is involved and they will end up being your publicity for you because they will bring some other new people along. Of course there is more to starting a new initiative than this, but it is a start. In chapter 8 we will look at this in more detail, but this should give you a discussion base.

THINK, WRITE AND PRAY

Stop for a moment and draw a diagram of all the families you have any form of contact with: for instance, you may have contact with only one member of the family. Write a list of these people and next to each one the other family members you know about. Draw a diagram with your name in the centre of the page and round you a circle of family people you know. Then out through them draw a line of other family members they represent. Count up all the children you have direct or indirect contact with. Pause and pray for each of them by name – potentially they are the members of your brand new children's evangelism initiative!

Group Focus:
thinking through specific ideas for evangelism with children

Focus in

Look back at the list of different forms of evangelism at the start of the chapter, then at the suggestions for different types of evangelism in the 'church' section:

- Each person in the group should choose one or two types of evangelism that they feel would be right, and share it with the group, giving reasons for their choice.
- Pray together.

Local needs

Look back through the chapter and share the thoughts you have had. You may find some of the following questions useful:

- What do you see as the main needs of children in your area?
- How do your ideas fit in with the current children's work in your church?
- What could your existing church families contribute to children's evangelism?
- What are the resources – people, money and support – available at the moment?
- What level of support can you expect from your local schools?

Starting points

There is another way of looking at evangelism – by using seasonal occasions to make a link with the children and families you want to reach. Think how you could use these opportunities within your own church programme:

- **New Year** Using the theme of 'a new start' gives you the opportunity to explain the possibility for a real new start when God makes us a new creation. How will you present this to children who are not yet a regular part of the church?
- **Lent** Use the theme 'pause to think'. Many churches invite people at this time to special groups which meet to look at Christianity. Could there be appropriate groups for children and teenagers?
- **Mothering Sunday** Use the theme of 'serving others'. This is an opportunity to introduce the 'servanthood' aspect of Jesus' life and how he took on the role of serving

the unimportant, rejected and 'forgotten' people in order to reveal God. How can you use this theme and this occasion to bring the good news to children in your community?

- **Palm Sunday** This could be the time to take to the streets! Lead a time of singing and praise in your local streets and take the opportunity to explain that Jesus came to die. What could you include in your procession to attract, inform and challenge children?
- **Good Friday** In what ways could the sombre mood of this day be reflected in what is worn, what is eaten, what is said and done so that children can enter into it? It is helpful for children, even those 'inside' the church, to experience the darkness of Lent and Good Friday in order to enter fully into the joy and celebration of Easter.
- **Easter Day** Explore new, creative ways of showing the joy and triumph at Easter so that children who are not regularly in your church can appreciate it. A party may be appropriate.
- **Pentecost** The festival of Pentecost is easy to celebrate – although hard to teach accurately. What could you do with the themes of fire and wind to involve the children of your church in the excitement of this festival? How could you do it so that they want to invite their friends to come too?
- **Harvest** This 'traditional' way of giving thanks and remembering people who do not enjoy all the riches we have can have a strong family focus. How could you use some of the traditional ways of giving, eating and celebrating the harvest to present God's gospel to children?
- **Advent** Celebrating Christmas without celebrating Advent is like not knowing that your birthday is tomorrow – you are cheated of the anticipation. Think through how you could involve those outside the church in anticipating Christmas rather than simply involving them in Christmas itself.
- **Christmas** Look at the ideas you have talked about for Advent and think of the natural ways there would then be to go on and celebrate Christmas with those who do not yet know Christ.

You could suggest that the members of the group go away and pray about this.

THE TEAM

Gathering the team

Working in a team is fun. The relationships that develop between those who work together in evangelism is unique. These relationships grow through traumas and battles. They grow through seeing signs of God at work in children and in each other. They grow through learning to live in a constant attitude of prayer and spiritual preparation; through surviving those days where, without God and his strength, all would be lost. All these things produce relationships which are like gold. In this chapter we shall look not only at the way in which to choose, collect and train a team, but also at the demanding job of leading a team. What follows is mainly aimed at the potential leader of a team.

Leading a team

One important decision to make at the beginning is who is going to lead the team. Someone must be the leader, otherwise decisions will go round in circles and questions will never be answered. Perhaps, as you are reading this book, it is you? Or you yourself may not be good at leading, but do you have a good idea about who could do it?

It is the leader who will need to spend time on their own with God, preparing, asking him to equip them for this demanding and exciting task; praying through the decisions about who to work with; allowing the Holy Spirit to begin to work in their imagination as they start to think through all the issues.

The leader needs a co-leader. This person will be a personal support – someone they can laugh with, be honest with and pray with, without reserve. Finding the right person for this support role should happen early on in the process, before the team is in place; even before they share their ideas with other people. The support is there so that the leader does not become isolated and spiritually vulnerable in their leadership.

The leader needs a team. The team you gather round you should not all be like you – that would make a weak team. Jesus does not break down the differences between people but bridges them. There will be some tough times as you work with people who are very different from you. The strong and mature leader will recognize that these tough times are not simply because others are human and sinful but because the leader is, too!

Sharing responsibility. It is important to recognize that, from the moment you take over the leadership of the team, you can ask people to take responsibility for all sorts of practical arrangements, work and decisions. But you can never hand over spiritual leadership. From the moment you step into leadership you are required to pray deeply, live a godly life, exercise faith in prayer and decisions, look for growth in yourself and in the members of the team. Challenge yourself about being a safe person for others to follow; to be a leader you should have already learnt to follow with grace and obedience. Those who are uncomfortable and argumentative when others lead them should never be leaders themselves – they have not learnt the necessary basic lessons.

Making mistakes. Once you are a leader your growth in leadership can be quite traumatic – because it is so public! We have all been taught that we learn from our mistakes, but this doesn't make us feel any better about making them. The team you lead will sometimes see you make mistakes. Many of them will feel encouraged by your mistakes because they will realize that you are also on a learning curve, just as they are. Some of them may be fairly rough with you about your mistakes simply because they have taken the brunt of it or because they have never been in leadership positions themselves and don't realize the pressure the leader is under.

Mistakes happen because:

- decisions have been made too quickly
- responsibility for work has not been delegated to others properly
- the obvious, rather than the pertinent, decision was made
- the leader reacted to the situation rather than to the people involved
- the leader forgot they were a spiritual, not a secular, leader.

READ AND REFLECT

Read 1 Timothy 4. Look at what Paul tells Timothy to value in himself and in others:

- godliness (verse 7)
- training to be godly (verse 7)
- spiritual fitness (verse 8)
- devotion to godly living (verse 12)
- recognition of own gifts (verse 14)
- wholeheartedness in practising the gifts (verse 15)
- time to practise the gifts (verse 15).

READ

Read Ephesians 5:21 – 6:9. What should be the attitude of followers of Christ?

THINK

As you look at these lists, you may feel that you are being asked to aim for the impossible! But remember, God is already at work in your church and he is working in people so that they are ready to work for others. Many people think of children's work as something which anyone

can do. In fact, even when you are helping a child to wash their hands or to find their shoes, you are actually modelling the Christian life to them – you are introducing them to Jesus.

Who are the people in your church who:

- are modelling Jesus to you?
- are keeping spiritually fit by reading God's word and spending time in prayer?
- have recognized the gifts God has given them and are using them with generosity?
- have time, or who are prepared to make time, in order for other people to hear about Jesus?
- are following Jesus with a humble heart?
- will strengthen a team and not divide it?

You will see that there is nothing in this list which specifically mentions people who are good with children. Why is this? It is because the first qualities to look for in children's work are the *spiritual* ones. Many of the people you will have thought of will already know that they are good with children, but others may only find this out to their surprise as they join a team for children's evangelism. This is a risk you can afford to take – but you cannot risk people who are good with children but spiritually poor.

Training a team

First of all, think through the following before inviting individuals to join a team for children's evangelism:

- **Be clear** about what is involved – what are you asking them to do: a one-off, a series or a regular event?
- **Inform** the individual so they can make a good decision – write out your ideas and plans for evangelism before you talk to them: they can read this while they pray and consider their answer.
- **Offer training** – don't ask people to come along and 'learn on the job'. Offering training is affirming; it is showing the person that you think they are worthwhile and that the job you are asking them to do is an important one. Offering training well ahead of time will help the person to imagine what the job will be like and to prepare for it.

By training the team for evangelism – perhaps by going through this book together – you are aiming for three characteristics:

- **strength** – you need a strong team because you are going to be doing a demanding and adventurous job together. A team's strength is in what it has in common – a relationship with Jesus, love for his word and concern for children would be three common threads to make your team strong.
- **wealth** – you need a 'rich' variety of people on the team. If they are all the same – or all like you – the team will be impoverished. Encourage each team member to be happy and open about what gifts they are offering. Assure them that you do not want them to be like someone else but simply to be themselves.
- **growth** – you need a team of people who are flourishing: people who want to grow in their own relationship with God and with each other. Part of that growth will happen

as you work together and also as you see God working in the lives of children through you.

When you plan training, the programme should cover these aspects of your team:

- **heads** – they will need to think about what they are going to do. They will need to understand the gospel, the children they work with, the process they will be going through
- **hearts** – they need to feel excited about the possibilities of what they are doing, stirred by the difference the gospel can make to children, however small, and thankful for their own faith before they start
- **hands** – they need to be confident about the role they are going to play. They may have never spoken to a group before, or organized a craft session or kept a group of children sticking to the rules in a game. These may all be new skills that they need to learn.

Group Focus:
how the leader can get the best from the team – and how the team can get the best from their leader

Leading

Look at these ten suggestions for helping the leader limit their mistakes. What would you add to the list in order to get the best from the leader of your team?

- Choose the team only after much prayer and reflection.
- If you have only worked in a team in a secular setting before, remind yourself how different this will be.
- Make sure that any practical arrangements still allow members of the team opportunities to gain the spiritual support they need – for example, do not allow meetings to clash with home groups or a church service.
- Keep your main aim for the event continually in your mind.
- Set yourself the personal challenge to focus on prayer in a way you have never done before.
- Keep your own standards of godliness high.
- Be realistic about yourself, about others – and about God.
- Provoke your own hunger for training – don't think of it as simply being for other people.
- Help individuals on the team to assess their own spiritual gifts and training needs.
- Assess the training needs of the team as a whole.

Training

How will you receive training for evangelism? Talk together about practical ideas of the ways in which training could be given to you and to the wider group of people who will become involved in these activities. Make a list of the ways in which you need training, the times when you could be available to be trained and the people you know of who could come to give you the benefit of their experience.

Growing

Look back on the stages of growth in your own understanding of the gospel:

- How did you each come to own the faith for yourselves?

- How did you each start to recognize that you had a desire in your heart for others to find out about Jesus too?
- Who trained you in evangelism or modelled children's evangelism to you?
- What do you see as your own personal need for training at the moment?
- What are you praying God will do in your life as you become involved in evangelism with children?

Praying

Talk together about prayer for your evangelism with children:

- What happens when people pray?
- What kind of prayer are you each comfortable with?
- When is the best time for the team to meet in order to pray?
- Are there other people who could be encouraged to pray for you and for this venture?
- What sort of things will you be praying about?

DOING EVANGELISM

Proclaiming the good news of Jesus Christ to people who have never realized that they need to hear it is hard work. No matter where you live and what the children are like in your area, it can be tough and apparently unrewarding. But we are involved in evangelism because of who Jesus is and because of what the Bible says. So we know:

- we proclaim the gospel because it is true
- we proclaim the gospel appropriately for a person because we really want them to understand
- we proclaim the gospel even though there is never a guarantee of success – if it seems to fail we will then try another way.

Facing the challenge

Telling the good news takes a lot of preparation. Even personal one-to-one sharing of the gospel requires the Christian to know their faith and have an ability to put it into words which make sense. It is a huge challenge for an adult who is faced with a group of children and wants to explain the Christian faith in such a way that it not only makes sense but also elicits an appropriate response.

Sometimes, when faced with that challenge, churches tend to look round, realize that they have no one who can do it and give up! But this is a skill that can be learned. This is why the whole team will benefit from training. Those who are going to lead workshops, or play games, or sit on the floor in small groups with children will all have the same aims; they want the children to enjoy themselves thoroughly; and they will be looking out for opportunities to chat about Jesus. For most children, these sort of groups will be the ideal opportunities to ask questions.

Some Christians think it is easy to work with children, and that anyone can explain the gospel to children without any preparation because children cannot understand very much. That is not true! Children are not as advanced as adults because they have not lived so long, but this does not mean that children are stupid nor superficial. Quite the opposite! Children have not become cluttered up with much that fills an adult life. They think deep thoughts and can sustain them over a long period of time. If you

teach children a shallow half-truth about Jesus, they will find it unsatisfying and disappointing. They need to know and be satisfied by the whole truth about God, just as an adult does. We need to make sure that we can give this to them using a vocabulary which they can understand and drawing on illustrations which are within their experience.

Proclaiming the gospel to children is hard work and will take a lot of effort and preparation. You may need someone to visit your church to help you to think through how to do it. You may have one person in your church who does it well and who could help others to do it. Either way, it's worth doing because without hearing the gospel, children have missed the chance to make up their minds about Jesus.

The way in

There are lots of God-activities that you can use to support the proclamation of the gospel. It is important to understand that none of these are 'jam around the pill' but all of them will help children to focus on what you want them to understand. Doing these activities will mean that when you have something to talk to the children about, they will already be thinking about it before you start.

There are five components that seem to form a natural context for children:

- music
- drama, art, poetry
- Bible teaching/storytelling
- opportunities to respond
- workshops.

If you think about your own preferred context for hearing the Bible you will see that you have similar options. The first two – music and drama, art and poetry – can be seen as aspects of worship, which is one way in to God. The Bible teaching/storytelling and response can be seen as our 'core' teaching; and the workshops are a way in which children can explore God's truth through their own creativity. *All* of these activities, when taken together, are ways of communicating the gospel. Children are people, just like us, and in these different 'components' we find different ways of learning about God.

Music

Music is used in so many different ways: to set a scene in a film, or a mood in a shop or restaurant, to calm people in a waiting room or departure lounge, or to welcome people to a party. Music is important to all of us and we all respond to music, even if we are hardly aware that it is playing.

We need to use music thoughtfully as we work with children. We need to choose wisely the music which will welcome them as they arrive; the music we play for them to sing or listen to at the beginning to set the scene. Then we need to use care when we choose the music to sing before or after a talk. We need to listen to the music and to think through the words which are being used. We need to check that the words express truth correctly – because the words will always be remembered if they are set to good music. The words will either undermine the teaching we have given or underline it.

Drama, art and poetry

There are other ways we can express our thoughts to God. Here are ten ideas – these may spark off your imagination for more:

- **Drama** – it takes a lot of time to write good scripts and rehearse in order to put something across clearly and well, but it is worth it. Children are attentive and they will remember what they saw and heard.
- **Mime** – a large mime screen can be made out of a double sheet and fixed easily to a frame of wood. Behind this, drama is far less complicated – but still needs careful planning and rehearsal. As long as a good strong backlight is used, shadow mime can be innovative and exciting.
- **Demonstration** – children can watch an

activity which will then be used to illustrate some teaching. This can be very effective – for example, we invited a potter to make a pot, someone to arrange a beautiful display of flowers, someone to make things out of blown eggs, someone to bring a baby fox and live chicks. Each of these was later used in the teaching in a specific way.

- **Performance** – if you have someone in your congregation who has a short but relevant story from their own lives, and can tell it in a fascinating and engaging way for children, work with them to prepare to tell it to children. Many children are fascinated by what really happened to people long ago. (Remember to check that the story is really going to illustrate what you have to teach and not detract from it!)
- **Silence** – this can be used to good effect with children, so long as it is not used too often or sustained for too long. The use of silence in worship is something from which children really benefit.
- **Dance** – many children now experience dance in different forms in their schools; not all of them will want to be involved. Ensure that children who choose simply to sing and not to move are comfortable. There will always be some children who really love it; you could use a small group to help the group worship as they all sing.
- **Poetry** – children will vary in their experience and appreciation of this too, but you can increase their understanding and handling of poetry in the way you use it. Perhaps you could start by using a funny poem and then introduce more serious, thought-provoking ones as they get to know you better.
- **Reading aloud** – not everyone has this particular skill. Choose people who have clear diction and read in an interesting way, and who can engage with an audience. You could combine this with something visual like drama or beautiful photos enlarged on to an overhead projector or stuck up on to the wall as they read. You will find suggestions for word signs at the end of this book that can be used by the children to help them remember what they hear (see page 48).

- **Reciting the Bible by heart** – some older people often have this skill, but again, check that they can engage with their audience: they should have good eye contact with the children and hold their attention in the way they tell the passage. Ask them to hold a Bible in their hand since this will help to make it clear where the text comes from. Reciting enables children to listen to the Bible as it really is, rather than only ever through someone else retelling it.
- **Pictures** – a child's world is very visual, and any work with children includes the challenge to be as visual as possible. You may have the resources to use a video projector or an overhead projector, a television and video. You may simply be able to use large posters or enlarged personal photos. Whatever your setting, remember that children will always notice beautiful things – or the lack of them!

Bible teaching and storytelling

Although the Bible is not simply a storybook, much of its truth and teaching is contained in Bible stories. This means that for storytellers there is a wealth of material. The gifts of a storyteller can always be honed further, so whether you are just beginning to grow that gift or have used it for years, here are some helpful tips:

- Watch professional people who use storytelling on TV. Look at the expressions on their faces, the movements of their hands, the way they lean towards and away from their audience to create different reactions, and the way in which they use pictures or other supports and aids.

- Listen to the tone and pitch of their voice. Find out how they use their voice to indicate a change of scene, an increase in excitement, amazement or fear.
- Copy as many of these skills of storytelling as possible. Read stories out loud from books and tell them from memory, making the most of as many skills as possible.
- Experiment with real children as often as possible. Skills grow stale and techniques are

forgotten very easily. By using the gifts you have on a regular basis, the skill will grow.

When you are using storytelling as a vehicle for teaching Christian truth, be sure that you know the truth you want to teach. For example, you may have a sentence that you will repeat at various times throughout the story like a refrain; and the children will learn this as you tell the story, simply from hearing it several times. The sentence could also be used in other activities: in craft, or by adults who are leading other parts of the programme.

As you prepare, remind yourself that this story really happened to real people. It fitted into its place in history and it stayed in the minds of the people who witnessed it to such an extent that they bothered to write it down. Pray that the Holy Spirit will make the event more and more real to you as you study and prepare it. God was there at the time so pray that by the time you have completed your preparation it will feel as though you were there at the time, too. If you are doing your job properly, children will never be bored by hearing the Bible nor will they feel let down when they read the actual Bible account later for themselves. (Note: if the Bible does not give certain details that you feel are important for retelling the story, be very wary of introducing that extra material without making it clear that you are doing so.)

If you are using props or visual aids to supplement your storytelling, make sure you practise using these beforehand!

If not, you could find that all the hard work you have put into Bible preparation has been lost because the picture fell down or was upside down on the overhead projector. It often works well simply to use an object or a picture to set the scene at the beginning and then to tell the story and follow it with another picture or object to underline truth at the end. In this way, you can concentrate on the material you have prepared and communicate it in as vivid and memorable way as possible without being hampered.

Opportunities to respond

Whenever people are challenged about spiritual matters they need time to think and time to react. Few things are more frustrating than to be deeply challenged about the personal implications of something in the Bible – but to be given no opportunity to respond. Our traditional church services have Bible teaching after singing, prayer and reflection but often allow no time for response afterwards.

Children also need time to respond, and some suggestions of what an appropriate response might be. For example, time to respond may be given in the form of music to listen to, or a short time of silence with some indication of the way they might pray. One of the leaders may pray out loud for them and ask them to talk to their leader about what they have prayed. These are quite conventional, expected response forms. But there are other ways, too: can you think of a form of response that is directly linked into the Bible teaching you have given?

THINK

Take this example of an imaginative response to a Bible story: let's suppose you have told the children the story of God's people being brought out of Egypt through the Red Sea. The response time might involve a huge piece of blue cloth held up while people sing. Anyone wanting to make the response 'I want to be God's person living the way he wants me to live' can walk under the cloth while they sing. Very simple but very effective! Or let's suppose you

have told the story of the people of God going into the Promised Land with Joshua. For a response you could have huge footprints cut out of paper and invite children during a song to come to stand on a footprint as a way of saying 'I want to go God's way with Jesus'. Then finish with a prayer while they stand there.

The idea for the response needs to be simple and children need to be given the choice. They must be able to choose not to do it. However simple the idea, please take their response seriously, by offering further opportunity to explore it by, for example:

- giving them something that will remind them of what they have done
- referring to it at another time
- suggesting a particular person they could go to chat to later on, if they have made this response.

This is not in order to trap children into a deeper position than they are ready to go with God. Not at all! It is simply that they need to know that however small a step they take towards God, God knows and cares about it – and so do we.

REMEMBER

If you are one of the adults who will offer to chat to children after the event, there are important points to remember:

- Make sure that the child can speak easily without fear of other adults or children overhearing.
- Make sure you are in a place where other people can see you easily so that both you and the child feel safe and relaxed.
- Listen carefully to the child and let them take the lead with either their questions or their statements.
- Affirm the child and assure them of God's love for them.
- Be ready to encourage the child to pray.
- Be ready to pray with the child.

Workshops

Children are very creative people. They think and learn by doing rather than by hearing. So far, we have talked about the truth they are going to learn from music, art, drama and poetry and direct Bible teaching. Another way in which they engage with the Bible truth is by using their own creative gifts and skills. A choice of workshops, used for part of the time they are meeting together, will help them explore Bible truth in a deeper way.

THINK

What are the benefits of offering children a choice of workshops?

- **Using your team's skills.** The variety of workshops you can offer to children is almost limitless; you may find you have a wide variety of skills in your team. Using these will make the individuals in your team feel valued, so find out what interests they represent – you will find out all sorts of things about people you thought you knew quite well! Think together of a good list of simple workshops to run.
- **Opportunities to talk and listen to children.** Workshop ideas need to be simple – if they are too complicated the adults' concentration will be on getting a good result rather than listening and talking to children. The informal setting of the workshop allows some 'deep' conversations, without pressure.
- **Involve more members of your church.** This is a chance to involve people who have never thought of working with children before.
- **Share your results.** The 'end-products' of the workshops could be placed on view in the church when the regular congregation meets and thus spread the impact of the evangelism with children to people who are not actually doing it.
- **Reveal God as Creator.** Doing workshops helps children to realize that God is not concerned simply with 'religious' things but with the whole of our lives. We reveal a family likeness when we use our creative gifts. Children need to know that they are children of the heavenly Father – the Creator God.
- **Reminders.** Children may well remember this workshop long after the event, and it will remind them that they have been involved in the life of your church – it should also remind them of what they have heard and learnt.

DO

Make a list of the workshops and ask people to run them. You will need at least two leaders in each group of eight children. Give the leaders time to plan and organize their workshop and check with them ahead of time what they are doing and what equipment they will need. They will need to know what budget they have and how to claim their expenses – give them as much information as possible. The most important thing is to make sure that they know what you will be teaching from the Bible on the day of their workshop. Then they will realize that the aim of the workshop is to underline and explore the teaching. Their workshop has a spiritual aim that runs alongside their creative aim.

Group Focus:
teaching the Bible effectively using creative ideas

The challenge is not just to talk about being creative with children, but to be creative ourselves in our worship of God, in our understanding of the gospel, and in our teaching and sharing of the gospel. Here are some activities to help the team think through some of the aspects covered in the chapter.

Worship God together, using creative ideas

This may feel strange at first – ask someone in your team to suggest two new ways of worshipping God for this time; ask someone else to use two other ideas each time you meet. In this way you will be building up the number of ideas you are happy to try together before you do them with children. Always focus on God and not on the idea – and if it goes wrong you can always try it again next time!

Think through the gospel you are wanting to communicate

First, make a list of the important facts of the gospel; then read Romans 5:1-11 and check your list.

- Is there anything on your list which is not mentioned in this passage?
- Is there anything in the passage which you have left out of your list?
- Try to think how you would put each item on your list into words for an eight-year-old.
- Which words on your list or in the Bible passage would not be appropriate for a child?
- How would you expect children to react to each of these statements of truth?

God the Creator

Read Genesis 1:1 – 2:3. Here we see the Creator God at work, and we stand at the moment when humankind was created.

- How would you introduce the Creator God to children who had never met God before?
- How would you describe the work done in creation?
- How would you describe the work God does day by day in sustaining the world?
- How would you encourage a sense of amazement in children about being a person of God's creation?
- How would you make sure that whenever children came to your evangelistic events they were reminded of the Creator God and learnt to worship him?

Think creatively about workshops

- Brainstorm all the possible workshops which children might enjoy. Be as adventurous in your suggestions as possible. Don't just go for the obvious ones!
- Think about the building where your evangelism is to take place; and imagine the different places where workshops could happen; make a plan of the building and write in the names of the workshops you could run.
- Make a list of the people who might run workshops and the number of children appropriate to each one (remember to check the adult/child ratio appropriate to the age-group).
- Encourage each other to feel excited about this; pray through the rooms of the venue together, using this as a way of imagining the workshops taking place.

FOLLOW-UP

A cautionary tale

The evening began much as any other on camp. We changed after our afternoon activities, washed up after the meal and went up to our dormitory to collect a Bible, notebook and pen. I sat that evening with my back to two big windows, facing the huge fireplace and panelled wall in the lounge of the old school. Behind me the hills and rivers, which had provided the delights of the day, were unable to distract me as I listened to the leader of our camp talk about the cross. I knew the material so well, and after thirteen years of being steeped in its teaching was familiar with the application – but this time it was different. Instead of listening to something that was for everyone else, I came to Christ and asked him to forgive my sins. The next morning I went to look for the leader who had given the talk. As I made my way across the landing I saw her running down the stairs and called out after her. She looked up and I shouted out to her that I had 'become a Christian'. She continued to run – presumably for the phone or another emergency – and the last thing I heard was, 'I'm really glad, Penny.' She never spoke to me about it later or checked up that I had spoken to another leader.

I struggled in my faith for years, partly, I think, because everyone assumed I would be well taken care of. I came from a Christian family and went to a good church. In fact no one ever sat down with me and helped me to sort out what my relationship with God had been for the last thirteen years and how it had now changed. I had always talked to Jesus, so what did I mean when I said that I had 'become a Christian'? I needed to see that the difficulty I had with giving in to God's love resulted from my rebellion towards my parents. Going God's way was like giving in to them and going their way, too – that was hard and did not get easier as time went by.

Of course, there were girls on that camp who had never before heard the story of the cross. One in our dormitory cried well into the night after hearing it because she had only grasped the bad news of sin and not the good news about forgiveness. She had no knowledge of the Holy Spirit, either, and so she was terrified to get up in the morning because she would only go and sin again. She had no context in which to set any of the teaching we had been given at camp, so the conversation she needed to have with a leader was very different from the one which I needed to have.

What and why?

That experience has shown me that following up the children we evangelize is very important, indeed essential. It is very easy to get to the end of a holiday club or some special outreach, and think that it's finished. It isn't! Not only that, the above story underlines the need for follow-up to be appropriate to the child.

We should always bear in mind the difference between the 'churched' and the 'unchurched' in our modern world. Children who come to church from church families know so much, which we can easily take for granted when we are working with them all the time. Their knowledge of the Bible, the Trinity and the church suddenly becomes vital breath when their lives are touched by the Holy Spirit. Conversely, this reservoir is largely empty when an unchurched child starts to grow in their relationship with God. However, all children need to know that there is more to following Jesus than they have yet found out, and they need to be excited about this.

Perhaps the evangelism you are planning with children is going to happen regularly and will follow up children in itself. Other forms of evangelism will need specific follow-up to ensure that each child knows what has taken place, and how to go on from there. Whether your evangelism is an annual or a weekly event, children need to know that you go on loving and caring for them when the event is over; and they need to be aware that what they know of Jesus will become more important in their lives.

Follow-up can take all sorts of different forms. Here are some ideas:

■ Invitations dropped in at their home for other events at the church – this is so that they know that you regard them in some way as belonging there.

■ Sending of cards at appropriate times of the year to mark birthdays, Christmas, etc.
■ Home visits; if these were a feature of your evangelism, you may decide to continue them.
■ Other events at your church which happen more regularly. These events, of course, need to be 'child-friendly' and suitable for 'unchurched' visitors. Whatever form it takes, your evangelism needs to be seen as part of a longer journey of faith, the beginning of a great relationship between the church and that child or family, not as an end in itself.

How and who?

The people who have been involved in your evangelistic events are the people who have begun to make real friendships with children, so

it would make sense if they are the ones who keep that friendship going afterwards. However, this is not always possible. Sometimes the people running special events are not the ones who are running the regular groups for children in your church. They may not be available for after-school clubs or Saturday morning groups which may be the form your follow-up takes. So:

■ It is important that planning for follow-up happens at the same time as you plan the main part of your evangelism. The people who are going to run the follow-up will then be able to visit the main events in such a way that children will feel they know them and parents feel they can trust them.
■ People responsible for follow-up need to make contact with the children immediately the main event has finished or as soon as the school holidays start (if the evangelism you are planning takes place regularly in term-time) so that there is no gap between the ending of the main event and the beginning of the follow-up.
■ An after-school club might be followed up with a Saturday morning club in the school holidays; or a holiday Bible club at the end of the holidays to gather the children together in order to restart the club. If your main event is a sports club on a Saturday morning during term-time, you might arrange special coaching on three mornings of the school holidays with other activities over the rest of the week.
■ If your main event is using the days leading up to Easter or Christmas with a special event in your church or local school then you might run 'reunions' regularly throughout the rest of the year. These need to use the same theme. In this way you would keep in contact with the children until the next main event the following year.
■ You may find at the end of your main event that there are children who are asking lots of questions about spiritual things. Perhaps they really want to grow a personal relationship with God through Jesus. In this case you may want to start a small group just for them where they can find out more.
■ A small group used as follow-up (as above)

might be linked in to your regular children's groups at church. In this case, you need to do more than invite the children. Think of a special way to invite them and welcome them into the group. The children who already attend that group will need help to welcome the new children properly.

- Whatever kind of follow-up you do, it is important that you prepare and publicize it as carefully as you did the main event. Do not undertake more than you can sustain. It's better to aim to have contact with each child once a month and achieve that than to aim for weekly contact and give up after a month.
- Ensure that the parents are kept as well-informed about the follow-up as they were about the main event. Make sure that in all these more informal contacts with children you are adhering to the Children's Act regulations and recommendations – you need to be safe and the children need to be safe. It is very easy to forget to be careful with a small group; if anything, it is more important (see page 48 for guidelines based on the Children's Act).
- Ensure that the follow-up is child-friendly and that contact with the child is organized in the context of their family.

All-age service

One of the ways in which your church can keep good on-going contact with children and their families is through a service that is for people of all ages (see page 48). Perhaps you have one already or perhaps you could start one as part of the new initiative you are taking with children and evangelism. An all-age service should be an expression of the all-age life of the church. It should be a bridge or first doorway into church life. Families coming into a service like this should find:

- **a simple but not embarrassing service.** Many of our services are complicated and depend on the worshippers being confident and knowledgeable about their faith to make sense of them. An all-age service needs to presume nothing and yet still be worthwhile. It needs to have one obvious theme and it

needs to be short. It can contain many of the things which express worship and which we looked at in the last chapter. It should be the sort of service where people have easy access to any books or words they need and where as much as possible is visual and memorable.

- **an understandable explanation of God's word.** Explaining the Bible to people of many different ages and types is never easy, but in fact there are only two main barriers to people understanding. These are *boredom* and *confusion* – a boring delivery by the speaker and a confusing array of out-of-date vocabulary! Here are some guidelines:
  1. Prepare the Bible passage so that you have some understanding of it – you may need to do this as part of a group. There are many accessible commentaries now available to help our understanding.
  2. Explain the passage in words which people can understand.
  3. Explain it in a way that catches and keeps children's attention.
  4. Aim to put across one simple point.
  5. Prepare the passage so thoroughly that you only take the amount of time you really need to talk about it.
  6. Involve the children where appropriate in actually doing something with you, rather than just listening to you.
- **a place where both children and adults are expected to be** – so that they know from the moment they come in that they are in the right place, where they have a contribution to make as well as something to receive. Those with very tiny children need to know the layout of the building and know what other rooms are set out for children if their toddler suddenly needs a break. They need to know where the toilets are and they need to be offered some hospitality either before the service or afterwards.
- **an opportunity to find out about the rest of the life of the church** – but without having to sit through a lot of notices which are really for the regular members. To go away with a welcome leaflet which summarizes what happens in your church, or to be given an invitation card for the one thing which you know is suitable for them, is

better than boring them with endless detail from the front of church.

- **a place where they can contribute as they grow in faith.** Too many people feel that they can only give something if they are clever, rich or good-looking, whereas God's church is for all his creation.

The all-age service in a church is often an excellent way to bridge the gap between a special event or series of events for children, and the rest of the life of the church. But you don't make a good all-age service simply by putting people of different ages into one service in a church – there is much more to it than that. So, if you see a regular all-age service as something which you plan to offer as a follow-up to your evangelism, now is the time to start planning it!

Home groups

Another excellent way of following up the children who have been to your main event is to run after-school home groups for children in homes of church members who live near the schools where the children go. You will need two leaders for each home group of eight children. One is the host and the other is the group leader – although they may both share the leading of the activities.

The running of the group is very simple:

- The children come straight from school, brought either by their parents or one of the leaders.
- They are given a drink and biscuit when they arrive, and while you set the scene: if you had a video of the main event they could watch a short excerpt; or use a poster, or theme song on a tape, instead.

If you wore a badge or a T-shirt for the evangelism, wear it now.

- To start, sing some of the songs that were used at the main event and play a game or do another activity that will introduce the theme for the day.
- Watch a Bible story on video. There are many now available which tell the story simply but in a captivating way.
- The leader can use a chat-sheet on a clipboard to help the children go through the story again. It might contain a quiz or a puzzle or a picture that will focus their discussion. The chat-sheet always focuses on the Bible story.
- Make time to pray through some of the things the children have been talking about.
- Make something which the children can take home to remind them of what they have learnt.
- The children all take home the craft activity and a copy of the chat-sheet, with a note to their parents telling them what they have been learning today and when the next home group meets.

With follow-up involving more than one home group, the material can all be prepared centrally as the groups can follow the same programme. But the challenge is to find leaders who are available after school.

One way to organize this kind of follow-up is to gather the leaders together once a month for coffee and go over the programme with them.

- Go through the chat-sheet and demonstrate the game and the craft.
- Explain what materials the leaders need to prepare and provide – some of them can be provided centrally.
- Give them invitations to fill in with the date and venue of their group.
- Encourage them to give out these invitations to parents and children.
- Make a list of the dates when the groups are going to meet, and where.

If there is more than one group, and they meet on different days, you can deliver the box with all the materials before the group meets, or tell them when to collect it from you. They then have time to prepare the group, run it and return the box to you for the next group meeting.

Home groups for children give an opportunity for quality contact with children through which they can learn about God within the intimacy of a home. The simple programme runs easily and, provided the right explanation and introduction is made with parents, most are happy – or even impressed – with the provision. But it all takes good initial planning and preparation. This may be something you want to think about as you plan your evangelism with children. It is important that all the recommendations of the Children's Act are adhered to in this provision (see page 48).

Materials

Whatever follow-up you are doing, you need to plan what the children are going to learn and explore during that process. It is as important a decision as deciding what to teach them during a main event of evangelism. There are some important principles to remember whenever you plan to teach children the Bible – whether in the main event, the follow-up groups or in your regular children's groups in your church.

1. What you teach needs to be true to the Bible. Many children do not have any knowledge of the Bible. They do not know what God has said, nor what God has done, nor do they know how God views them. Teaching the Bible to children is exciting: it is something that can open a doorway of possibilities for their own life and their family's lives. Coming into a relationship with God is something that will radically change how they see themselves and other people. So it is essential that those of us who are going to lead children in the church or in evangelism through the church need to get to know what we are teaching thoroughly. We need time to get to know biblical truth; and we need to make sure that we are allowing God to live that truth out through our own lives. This needs to happen before we ask him to speak to children through us. Children listen to what we say and they look at how we live: if the way we live contradicts what we say, they will stop listening to us.

2. How you teach children needs to be child-friendly. This sounds so obvious, doesn't it? So often the materials churches produce for children are not fun at all – often they are downright boring. Those of us who are going to lead children in the church, and through the church in evangelism, must get to know the child's culture for ourselves. I can never be a child again, and I will never know what it is to be a child now, but I can find out as much as I can. I can watch their TV programmes, buy their magazines, see their films, and listen to them. We need to change our emphasis from talking to listening. As their culture becomes more familiar, then we will be able to chat more easily to them and, when we teach the Bible, the illustrations and allusions we use will be theirs.

3. Be prepared to adapt materials to suit your children. There are many good materials which have been commercially produced, but it can be very frustrating, looking for something which is just right for the children of your area. Be prepared radically to adapt materials with your children in mind. That doesn't mean you have wasted your money or that the materials are poor, but simply that children from different areas are different. Alternatively, put together your own materials. Remember, either way:

- The Old Testament reveals the character of God really clearly – if children don't know God, then this can be a good place to start.
- Jesus needs to be specifically introduced to children. If we muddle Jesus up with the Old Testament stories, children become, rightly, very confused about the gospel message we are teaching.
- The New Testament stories can seem appealingly easy to teach, but they were written on the whole for people who knew the Old Testament. They therefore presume knowledge of the character of God that our children almost certainly will not have.

Group Focus:
follow-up activities so that evangelism produces long-term results

What sort of follow-up?

Think through together the kind of follow-up programme you might be able to run. Here are some questions that might help:

- How many leaders will be available?
- How many helpers will be available?
- What choice of venues do you have?

- What are the social habits of your local children?
- How has this to fit into your church diary?
- What is your long-term aim for evangelism in your church over the next five years?
- How do your follow-up plans fit into it?

Follow-up and existing groups

If the follow-up you are planning is to make a link between the children you already have in your church groups and the new children you are reaching with your evangelism, and you are aiming to grow the new and the established children together, look honestly at the regular provision for children in your church:

- How easy would a child from a non-church home find it to join in?
- Are there ways in which your plans may challenge the regular groups for children in your church so that they become better groups for newcomers?
- Are there ways in which your plans for evangelism will have an impact on leaders of these groups so that they grow and are encouraged in their work with children?
- Are you planning to use the evangelism to promote children's groups in your church generally, so that there is more support and prayer for them throughout the church?

Getting to know God better

Children, in both the established and the newcomers' groups, are getting to know God better by developing their relationship with Jesus and receiving the Holy Spirit. With the children in mind, but based on your own experience:

- Write down what you think God's character is like.
- Taking one characteristic at a time from your list, think which Old Testament story would teach it.
- Read through each Old Testament story you have thought of, to make sure that it does illustrate that characteristic.
- Record your list so that you can use it in the future when you are thinking about teaching the Bible to adults or children.
- Now go through the same list and think which stories of Jesus would illustrate that characteristic of God. Find each and read it through to make sure.
- Now pray through the list, thanking God for his character and for revealing himself in Jesus. Pray that this characteristic will be obvious in your own life as he lives in you. Pray for your local children that they will come to know God for themselves.

ALL GOD'S CHILDREN?

The following conclusions come from Chapter 8 of the Church House report *All God's Children?* They may be helpful in your thinking about children's evangelism in your area.

8 SUMMARY OF FINDINGS

(with questions for local churches)

8.1 The Working Party looked at the present situation facing children in society today. It recognized the enormous changes that have taken place since the Second World War, not least in the place that religion has within our culture.

8.2 It noted the serious decline in the churches' outreach to children since about 1955. In the 1950s the majority of our children were still encountering the gospel, half of them through Sunday schools. Today the situation has deteriorated, so that only about 14 per cent of our children encounter a church community.

How many children in your area have connections with local churches?

What percentage is that of the child population?

8.3 The churches tried, with some notable successes, to respond to the changing situation. New teaching material reflected changes in teaching styles in schools. Again with some conspicuous successes, family worship, with more informal liturgical patterns and greater involvement, became part of parish life. Churches moved their Sunday schools from afternoon to morning; some moved them to another day of the week. Parishes tightened up their baptism policies to give opportunities for parents and godparents to have some learning experience of the Christian faith.

How does your church seek to involve children?

What is the parish baptism policy?

8.4 These efforts, however, reached only those children whose parents were prepared to be involved themselves. Increasingly children were being marginalized from the Church.

8.5 The Working Party looked at the influences on youngsters today. It recognized that the vacuum left by the lessening of the Church's influence had been filled by other forces and messages. Some of these were good, many were not. It is certainly a fallacy to imagine that today's world is ideologically or morally neutral. It was also noted that childhood is being squeezed out, as children are pressured to share adult values and concepts.

What do you consider to be the major influences on the lives of children in your area today?

8.6 Changes in family life were noted. Higher standards of living are being financed by great debt. There are more families where both parents are financially employed, and this affects the time that the family can spend together. Increasingly many children are being brought up by one parent, whilst others are living with one natural and one step-parent.

What patterns of family life are to be found in your area?

What is the pattern of family life experienced by members of other faith communities in your area?

8.7 Today there is a marked increase in the number and range of out-of-school activities for children. Alongside this is an ever-increasing danger in the 'outside world', which leads to many children being transported to and from safe activities. Other children are left to fend for themselves in a world full of powerful temptations and dangers.

How do local children in your area spend their free time?

8.8 The power of television cannot be underestimated. It opens children to 'the ambiguous world of adult values and activities'. On the one hand, it can widen children's horizons, increase their knowledge, understanding and appreciation of the world and encourage compassion and generosity. But on the other hand, it can inhibit natural creativity, give a distorted view of reality, and introduce children to sex, violence and evil before they are emotionally able to cope with them.

What TV programmes do children watch?

How do you think those programmes affect them?

8.9 Commercial firms can exercise power and influence as they see children as targets for their marketing strategies. It is often children who decide what brand or product a parent should buy. Even toys play their part, encouraging children to build up collections, or enter a fantasy world where all is glamour and success.

8.10 Today's heroes are also used as part of a commercial and moral assault on our children. They are not simply idols, they are promoters of fashions, of activities, of attitudes.

Who are today's heroes for children?

What sort of lifestyle do they present?

8.11 Into this scenario the Working Party began to identify some signposts for the Church's own involvement.

AN EVANGELISTIC IMPERATIVE

8.12 Evangelism among children is not an option for Christians, but should lie at the heart of our life and witness.

8.13 There is a moral imperative here. If, for whatever reason, we choose to leave the evangelism of children until they are older, then the battle may already be lost. The

hearts and minds of our children are being forcefully moulded early in life.

8.14 There is a spiritual imperative. The kingdom of God belongs to children – all children – because they are who they are. God is for them. Thus they need to be helped to see that there is a God to whose kingdom they belong.

8.15 There is an ecclesiastical imperative. *Children in the Way* underlines that if the children are outside the Church, then those who are 'inside' are themselves impoverished. We need them as much as they need us.

How important is evangelism work among children in the life of your church?

What priority are you prepared to give it?

WHERE ARE THE CHILDREN WHO DO NOT COME TO CHURCH?

8.16 The answers need to be identified carefully, and the Church must assess in the light of its resources and abilities where and when evangelistic activity will be staged.

8.17 Almost all children belong to a family. The report highlights some problems as well as opportunities here. The fifth commandment challenges us to take seriously the concerns of parents and the family. How can the Church be faithful to the divine imperative to evangelize, and yet honour the child's family who may be non-believers or adherents of another faith? How can we harness a general parental willingness to support anyone who is doing something good for their children?

Given your answers to 8.6, how does this affect any strategy you might have for work with children?

Are there children of other faiths in the parish? If so, what ought your approach to be to them?

8.18 Nearly all children go to school and spend much of their most active time there. The Church has a long and honourable history of involvement in schools. Education, including Religious Education, is undergoing many changes which reflect changes in society. Much teaching is experientially based. There are growing numbers of children of other faiths and cultures, whose views need to be respected. Yet there is also a demand for schools to be answerable to society (and especially to parents), to give value for money, and to show that standards are improving. It is in this complex, specialized and changing world that the Church still has the freedom to work. But she needs to be vigilant, ensuring that her activities, be they individual or corporate, are both educationally motivated and pastorally sensitive.

To which schools do local children go?

What relationships exist between Church and schools?

8.19 Whilst children spend much time in school and at home, they are also involved in activities outside. For some there are organized activities. For others, however, there are more dangerous attractions on street corners, in amusement arcades or shopping centres.

What do local children do out of school time?

WHO IS TO DO THE EVANGELIZING?

8.20 Evangelism is the task of the whole Church. The Working Party did, however, identify a number of specific areas where we need to put some emphasis:

Clergy need to be trained both before and after ordination to develop skills of communicating with children individually and in groups. They need to be helped to relate to their local schools.

How can your clergy's ministry among children be supported and helped?

Christian parents need to be helped to contribute to the development and welfare not only of their own children but of others in the neighbourhood. They should be involved in the life and work of their children's schools.

What support is given to Christian parents?

Does your work with church-going children involve their parents?

Christians should be encouraged to give of their time and expertise in the service of children: to serve as governors of schools; to help run a club or organization; to help in school or out-of-school activities.

Which members of your church are involved in work with children?

Who else might be encouraged to become involved?

Christians should be encouraged, and should encourage others, to train as teachers.

Which members of your congregation are teachers?

Can you identify any people whom you might encourage to become teachers?

Christians should support the work being done by Christian organizations: the Mothers' Union, Scripture Union, the Church Pastoral Aid Society, the missionary societies, uniformed organizations and many others. They should also use diocesan resources that are available, especially the work of children's advisers.

Do you know about any national organizations working with your children in your area?

Do you know what resources they can provide?

Do you know what resources your diocese can offer?

> We need to recognize that denominational divisions are an irrelevance to children. We need to poll our resources and to work together with other Christians.

What are other churches doing in their work with children?

Do churches get together to share their work?

> **8.21** We recognized that many people are already working hard to build up our children, even though they may not work under the Church's banner. Christians should be prepared to be involved in and to support such work – e.g. pre-school playgroups, nurseries, uniformed organizations such as the Scouting movement.

What other organizations are there for your children?

Are any members of your congregation involved?

How do you show that you care about and support this work?

> **8.22** Other partners in this enterprise are the children who already belong to our churches. With help and support they can be most effective evangelists with their peers.

How do you encourage children to bring their friends?

> **8.23** The church congregation itself can do much to help. It should affirm and support teachers and all who work with children by prayer, encouragement and resources.

Do you pray regularly as a congregation for teachers, leaders and others working with children?

Do you pray for them, or for their schools and organizations, by name?

What resources do you as a congregation make available to them?

TIME AND PLACE ARE IMPORTANT

> **8.24** Research has shown that for many children Sundays are not the days when they are free to attend church-run activities. Sunday is often the family day, and increasingly other temptations are apparent – football, outings, etc. The stories told in the previous chapter show how an imaginative choice of time and a suitable venue can play a significant part in the success or failure of an enterprise. Sunday schools emerged from the social situation of their day. What is suitable for the social situation in which you find yourself?

Is Sunday still a 'free day' in your area, when church-organized activities can hope to find significant response?

What other times can be identified when local children can be expected to be free?

Do your present events happen in suitable premises?

THIS STYLE OF EVANGELISM IS IMPORTANT

8.25 Children seemed to gather around Jesus because he was an attractive character. He was then able to teach, to challenge and to encourage people to discover for themselves the truths of God's love. His attractiveness lay not in glitter and hype, but in his love for all whom he met and in his willingness to listen. He created a space in which they could find God for themselves.

8.26 What we have to offer must be similarly attractive.

Our Church, worship and people should have a strategy for helping people new to the faith to be introduced sensitively to the life of the Church.

What is your church's strategy?

Is it working?

We need a welcoming, well thought-out and sensitive baptism policy with appropriate after-care not only for those who have been baptized, but for all children and their families.

Does your parish baptism policy need reviewing?

We need to be part of the Church's wider outreach, caring, for example, for mothers with young children.

We need to welcome into our homes children and families who live around us.

We need to see the evangelization of children and their families as part of our own spiritual pilgrimage. It is not only what we can do for children, but what they can do for us.

What contribution do you think children make to the life of your church – and to you as individuals?

8.27 How we evangelize will need to be appropriate to the child. The insights of 'faith development' underline that both the approach we make to children, and the response we expect, must be appropriate to them.

8.28 How we evangelize will need to be appropriate to the particular area in which we minister. Communities, clubs and groups should reflect the needs of local children.

METHOD OF EVANGELISM MUST BE APPROPRIATE

8.29 Somewhere, somehow, the Christian story needs to be told. We need to be with the children where they are. We will attempt to show them by what we do and are that we care for them and for their needs. But the story needs to be told and learned, and children need to be encouraged to respond. Suitable people and suitable material need to be identified.

Whose task is it to tell the Christian story to children?

What resources do you/will you make available for this work?

Have you used the advice and resources available through your diocesan children's adviser?

8.30 Churches will also want to discover how the link can be made between evangelistic work in the home, in school and in the community on the one hand, and with the worshipping community on the other. They will have to ensure that what the children experience when they come into the worshipping community is a fair reflection of what they have experienced of Christian care and teaching outside.

What are your strategies for linking children in clubs and groups with the worshipping community?

Is your church welcoming to children and young families?

How can you improve matters?

All God's Children?

Individually we lack direction,
but, as a family, we have protection,
a balance that prevents us going wrong
too often and, if sometimes, not for long!
And no one needs to feel that he or she has to take sole responsibility:
We're all involved – we each need one another,
mother needs child and child depends on mother,
the same is true for father, sister, brother.
So, each supplying what the others lack,
together we can trace the narrow track
that leads from childhood to maturity,
from earth to heaven – and what we're meant to be.

(*Nigel Forde*, Children in the Way *video*)

THE GOSPEL IN A NUTSHELL

Have you thought through how you would explain the gospel to children – how you would tell them the big story of the whole Bible? It's worth having a try.

Here's one example:

The gospel is the story of a God who, at the beginning of time, made people who were like himself – they had minds which could think the way God thought, they had mouths which spoke the way God spoke, they had hands which did the things which pleased God and they had feet which walked where God would want them to walk. So God and the people he had made were best friends – because you are best friends with those people who think like you, speak like you and want to do the things which you want to do.

But one day the enemy of God whispered into the ear of one of the people God had made and for the first time on this planet there was someone whose thoughts were not God's thoughts. Her hand reached out to do something which God had said 'You're not to do that' and her mouth began to make excuses for what she had done, and the story ends in the Bible 'and that evening they heard the Lord God walking in the garden and they hid from him among the trees'. Their feet took them away from where God was. The Bible says that the gate of heaven slammed shut and death rippled down through all the generations onto all people.

Ever since that day, everyone born on this planet has struggled to think God's thoughts, has had mouths which do not speak God's words, has hands which do the very things which God has forbidden them to do and their feet lead them away from God. So to our minds, God had a problem – he could not change his laws because his laws reveal his own nature and that cannot change. But he loves the people he has made. He made them in order to enjoy their company and for them to enjoy his.

So God came to our planet himself. He was born a real baby. He learnt to crawl and toddle – he was a real child, a real teenager, a real adult. But his mind only thought God's thoughts, his mouth only spoke God's words. His hands only did those things which God

would do and his feet only went where God would go. And people hated him. They strung him out on a cross and they tortured him slowly to death. God's enemy thought he had won – of course he did. Here was God on a cross – God dying! But death can only keep hold of those who have done wrong and Jesus had never done wrong. So he broke the power of death, he strode out from the tomb, he gave his disciples the shock of their lives and he has never died again since that day. He went back to heaven and left the gate wide open.

Since that day anyone can come to God for forgiveness – *any of us* of any age, or race, or creed, or background. And because Jesus died and Jesus lives again, God forgives us for the wrong thoughts we have had and the wrong words we have spoken, our wrong actions and the wrong places we have been. The Bible says that when God forgives me it is just as though I never sinned, so death cannot keep hold of me either. On the day when my family mourns my death I will be more alive than I have ever been before. I'm on my way to heaven!

And in the meantime God fills me with his Holy Spirit and, very patiently, day after day, he is teaching my mind to think God's thoughts, he is teaching my mouth to speak God's words, he is teaching my hands to do the things he wants them to do and he is teaching my feet to go where he wants them to go. A wonderful story!

Growing in Faith series

Three books for all those involved in children's evangelism. The books work together and complement each other, providing a 'head, heart and hands' approach to the subject of child faith development. Written by experts in their field, the series will equip churches with a comprehensive training resource for children's workers.

Children Finding Faith: *Exploring a child's response to God*
Rev Dr Francis Bridger

This revised, expanded version of a popular book examines accepted studies of child development alongside the theological issues relating to children. Children Finding Faith follows the development of two children from birth to adolescence, charting the characteristics of their emotional and spiritual growth. New chapters look at social context, the practical implications of children's work and worship.

£6.99, B format pb, 224 pp   1 85999 323 0 (SU)   1 902041 10 0 (CPAS)

Bringing Children to Faith: *Training adults in evangelism with children*
Penny Frank

This training manual will enable you to think through the principles of good practice for evangelism with children, and implement them in your children's work. In workbook format, Bringing Children to Faith contains photocopiable pages and suggestions for group discussion and activity. Use this resource to plan a series of workshops for your church children's team, a training day or to help you as you develop a whole church strategy for children's evangelism.

£7.50, A4, 48pp   1 85999 410 5 (SU)   1 8976 6093 6 (CPAS)

Mission Possible: *Ideas and resources for children's evangelism*
Various

Mission Possible is a ready-to-use resource book full of ideas and activities for use with children. Arranged in age-group sections, ranging from crèche through to early teens, activities are relevant to children's age and level of development. Drawn from the experience of Scripture Union and CPAS children's workers, these tried and tested activities will enable you to put into practice some of the ideas outlined in the other two books.

£7.50, A4, 64pp   1 85999 411 3 (SU)   1 902041 05 4(CPAS)

You can obtain any of the above books through your local Christian bookshop, via christianbookshop.com or (in the UK) direct from:

Scripture Union Mail Order PO Box 764 OXFORD OX4 5FJ Tel: **01865 716880** Fax: 01865 715152
CPAS Sales Athena Drive Tachbrook Park WARWICK CV34 6NG   Tel/24 hour voicemail: **01926 458400**

For overseas sales, contact your national Scripture Union office.

Resources from CPAS and Scripture Union

From CPAS

CPAS Code

Growing in Faith Series (CPAS/Scripture Union)

03157	Children Finding Faith	Francis Bridger
03158	Mission Possible	compiled by David Bell and Rachel Heathfield
18006	The ART of 3-11s	
18007	Who Cares?	Rachel Heathfield
30001	My Place in God's Story	Rachel Heathfield
18003	Time for Children	George Lihou
82010	Families Finding Faith	John Hattam
03576	Seen and Heard	Jackie Cray
18001	Groups Without Frontiers	Phil Moon, Penny Frank, Terry Clutterham

CPAS Sales, Athena Drive, Tachbrook Park, WARWICK CV34 6NG
Tel: (01926) 334242
24-hour Sales Ansaphone: (01926) 335855
E-mail: sales@cpas.org.uk
Web: www.cpas.org.uk

From Scripture Union

ISBN

Growing in Faith Series (CPAS/Scripture Union)

1 85999 323 0	Children Finding Faith	Francis Bridger
1 85999 411 3	Mission Possible	compiled by David Bell and Rachel Heathfield
1 85999 180 7	Working With Under Sixes	Val Mullally
0 86201 544 8	Help! There's a Child in My Church!	Peter Graystone
0 86201 906 0	The Adventure Begins	Terry Clutterham
0 86201 862 5	Become Like a Child	Kathryn Copsey
01 85999 096 7	Pick 'n' Mix: Over 100 ideas to create programmes for children of all ages	Judith Merrell
1 85999 219 6	Jump! Bible activities for your group aged 5-7	Zoë Crutchley and Veronica Parnell
1 85999 215 3	On your marks! Bible activities for your group aged 8-10	Lorna Sabbagh
1 85999 214 5	Pitstop: Bible activity ideas for your group aged 11-13	Steve Bullock
0 86201 544 8	A Church for All Ages: A practical approach to all-age worship	Peter Graystone, Eileen Turner
1 85999 202 1	Am I Beautiful… or what?! Outreach and ministry to people with learning disabilities	David Potter
1 85999 351 6	Generation to Generation: building bridges between churches and schools	Sue Radford et al

Holiday club material (5 day holiday club programmes):

1 85999 329 X	Go for Gold (book and video available)
1 85999 284 6	Megaquest: God's big plan for the world (book and video available)

Children's Bible reading resources:

Jigsaw (3 to 5 year olds) – 4 undated books

Join in – jump on! (5 to 7 year olds) – 6 books, each containing 50 days of Bible reading material.

Snapshots (8 to 10 year olds) – published quarterly.

One Up (for 11 to 14 year olds) – published quarterly.

SALT (Sharing and Learning Together) resources: SALT 3 to 4+, SALT 5 to 7+, SALT 8 to 10+, SALT 11 to 13+, SALT All-ages. A4 leaders and children's magazines published quarterly.

All of these resources are available from Scripture Union Mail Order, PO Box 764, OXFORD OX4 5JF
Tel: (01865) 716880 or from your local Christian bookshop.
E-mail: su.mailbox@lion-publishing.co.uk
Web: www.christianbookshop.com